Paul Cookson is the ⌐   ⌐
National Football Museum und also Poet 🝔 ⌐⌐⌐
Everton Collection at Liverpool Library. His football
poems have appeared on *Match of the Day*, Sky
TV, Radio 5 Live, Radio 2, talkSPORT Radio and the
World Service. He has written lots of football poems
about 1966, Everton and more – go to his website to
see them: www.paulcooksonpoet.co.uk. He once
held the World Cup and the 1966 ball, and he's met
some of his football heroes and written poems about
them. Paul still tries to play five-a-side football once
a week. Oh – and he goes round to loads of schools
with his poems and his ukuleles. Become a fan on the
Facebook page: Paul Cookson Poetry Fans.

'A natural!' 'Like a combination of George Best and
Pelé.' 'It was a privilege just to be on the same field
with this footballing genius.' These are just a few of the
things never said about **David Parkins**. His weediness,
together with his spindly legs and natural cowardice,
was enough to make him last pick in any team-
choosing. In the end, he ran away to Canada, where
he lives with his wife, Angie, his teenage daughter,
Hattie, and some cats. He spends his time drawing
pictures for books, magazines, newspapers and
comics. And he still can't kick a ball hard enough
to get   y, that
makes   alls!

THE WORLD at our FEET

Football poems chosen by
Paul Cookson

Illustrated By David Parkins

MACMILLAN CHILDREN'S BOOKS

First published 2010 by Macmillan Children's Books
a division of Macmillan Publishers Limited
20 New Wharf Road, London N1 9RR
Basingstoke and Oxford
Associated companies throughout the world
www.panmacmillan.com

ISBN 978-0-330-51086-8

A CIP catalogue record for this book is available from
the British Library.

Printed and bound in the UK by CPI Mackays, Chatham ME5 8TD

To Peter Evans at the National Football Museum, Belinda Monkhouse at The Everton Collection, Blue Kipper and the Sunday-night footballers

This anthology was edited in partnership with the National Football Museum.

Contents

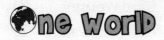 One World

One world
One cup
One moment

One aim
One hope
One dream

One chance
One game
One mission

One goal
One mind
One team

Daniel Phelps

We Are England

Once more we think of glory
Once more we dare believe
The dream of great victory
The prize we could achieve
But will we end the story
And flatter to deceive?

On paper the appearance
The players on our pitch
We have the right ingredients
But do we have the mix
To echo the experience
Of nineteen sixty-six?

The team that promises so much
This band of hyped-up men
Have failed to find that magic touch
Time and time again
They've stumbled in a state of flux
And fizzled in the end

The team that's nearly burned so bright
Must now relight that flame
Our time is now, our time is right
To stand up once again
We have the prize within our sight
If we but live up to our name

We are England, we are England
Champions we should be
We are England, we are England
Potential in our victory
We are England, we are England
It's time to live the dream anew
We are England, we are England
It's time to make those dreams come true

Paul Cookson

Reasons for Winning

Win it for the fans whose happiness will depend
  on it
Win it for the gaffer whose career may well end
  on it

Win it for the nurses and local authorities
Win it for the poor and ethnic minorities

Win it for the girl awaiting the operation
Win it for the firefighters racing back to the
  station

Win it for the late train and the overcrowded
  bus
Win it for Granny who can't understand the fuss

Win it for the dads who can't bear to lose
Win it for Brooklyn, Romeo and Cruz

Win it for kids in the playground, learning new
  tricks
Win it for old heroes at Wembley, the class of
  sixty-six

Win it for the expats, all the fans overseas
Win it for the viewers at home. Please.

Win it for the ordinary man in the street.
But above all, win it for yourselves,
You've got the world at your feet.

Reasons for Winning (*No Pressure*).

Roger McGough

Mexican Wave

A Mexican wave sweeps across the seats,

Fans of both teams leap to their feet;
Straightening bodies and arms stretched high,
A human ripple against the sky.

Chris Ogden

The World at our Feet

A great celebration of the World Cup elite
The great and the good all gather to meet
Come and join the party, come and take your
  seat
World Cup magic – the world at our feet

Watch all the drama in the African heat
Tactics to trick and skills that are neat
Brains and boots that flick or treat
Everyone's got – the world at their feet

A place where our heroes and legends can
  compete
Score the goals and win the prize and make
  our dreams complete
Hoping that the taste of victory will be sweet
World Cup winners – the world at our feet

We all hope that history will repeat
We all hope that we are going to beat
The rest of the world – then we all can greet
World Cup winners – the world at our feet

Paul Cookson

Song for the Kop

Three lions, roar with pride
Three lions, they won't hide
Three lions, brave and strong
Three lions, hear our song.

I'm ENGLAND till I die
I'm ENGLAND till I die
I know I am
I'm sure I am
ENGLAND till I die.

Three lions, blue on white
Three lions, rule all right?
Three lions, each a king
Three lions, hear us sing!

I'm ENGLAND till I die
I'm ENGLAND till I die
I know I am
I'm sure I am
ENGLAND till I die.

Three lions, in Africa
Three lions, going far
Three lions, here we go
Three lions, let them know!

I'm ENGLAND till I die
I'm ENGLAND till I die
I know I am
I'm sure I am
ENGLAND till I die.

David Harmer

It's a Small World . . . Cup

Nearly 200 countries in this world
Yet only 32 qualify.

From 7 continents on this planet
Only 2 have succeeded.

Since 1930 and in 18 finals
Just 7 teams have won.

The current overall score is a
    draw
South America 9 Western
    Europe 9.

Will the world be a **bigger** place
    in 2010
Or will it still be a small world . . .
    cup?

Ruth Underhill

Can We Have Our Ball Back, Please?

England gave football to the world
Who, now they've got the knack,
Play it better than we do
And won't let us have it back

Gareth Owen

The Commentator

Good afternoon and welcome
To this international
Between England and Holland
Which is being played here today
At 4, Florence Terrace,
And the pitch looks in superb condition
As Danny Markey, the England captain,
Puts England on the attack.
Straight away it's Markey
With a lovely little pass to Rooney,
Rooney back to Markey,
Markey in possession here,
Jinking skilfully past the dustbins;
And a neat flick inside the cat there.

What a brilliant player this Markey is
And he's still only nine years old!
Markey to Lampard,
Lampard to Markey,
Markey is through, he's through,
No, he's been tackled by the drainpipe;
But he's won the ball back brilliantly
And he's advancing on the Dutch keeper,
It must be a goal.
The keeper's off his line
But Markey chips him superbly
And it's a goal.
No!
It's gone into Mrs Spence's next door.
And Markey's going round to ask for his ball
    back,
It could be the end of this international.
Now the door's opening
And yes, it's Mrs Spence,
Mrs Spence has come to the door.
Wait a minute,
She's shaking her head, she is shaking her head,
She's not going to let England have their ball
    back.
What is the referee going to do?
Markey's coming back looking very dejected,
And he seems to be waiting . . .
He's going back,
Markey's going back for that ball!

What a brilliant and exciting move!
He waited until the front door was closed
And then went back for that ball.
And wait a minute,
He's found it, Markey has found the ball,
He has found the ball
And that's wonderful news
For the hundred thousand fans gathered here
Who are showing their appreciation
In no uncertain fashion.
But wait a minute,
The door's opening once more.
It's her, it's Mrs Spence
And she's waving her fist
And shouting something I can't quite
    understand
But I don't think it's encouragement.
And Markey's off,
He's jinked past her on the outside,
Dodging this way and that
With Mrs Spence in hot pursuit.
And he's past her, he's through,
What skills this boy has!
But Mr Spence is there too,
Mr Spence in the sweeper role
With Rover their dog.
Markey's going to have to pull out all the stops
    now.
He's running straight at him,

And he's down, he's down on all fours!
What is he doing?
And oh my goodness that was brilliant,
That was absolutely brilliant,
He's dived through Spence's legs;
But he's got him,
This rugged stopper has him by the coat
And Rover's barking in there too;
He'll never get out of this one.
But this is unbelievable!
He's got away
He has got away;
He wriggled out of his coat
And left part of his trousers with Rover.
This boy is real dynamite.
He's over the wall,
He's clear,
They'll never catch him now.
He's down the yard and on his way
And I don't think we're going to see
Any more of Markey
Until it's safe to come home.

Gareth Owen

The Drama

The drama, the excitement,
the beating of the drums,
the hopes of so many
when the championship comes.

The different colour strips,
the games under lights,
the nerves you will suffer
when it's match night.

The penalty awarded
to the other team.
The striker you weren't sure of
playing like a dream.

The swaying of the fans,
the singing and the shouts,
the prayers when your team's
about to be knocked out.

The handball the referee
won't give, despite the crowd.
The howl from the supporters
when a goal is disallowed.

The injuries, the tears,
the dreams and the fears,
and after it's all over –
there's another four years.

Jill Townsend

Every Tribe will Be There

A defender from Manila
A referee called Phil
A midfielder from Italy
A striker from Brazil
A fan from Barcelona
A physio from France
An old lady from Israel
(When they score, she'll dance)
A manager from Senegal
A reporter from Spain
A man who's been to ten World Cups
(And now he's back again!)
A linesman from Denmark
An official from Berlin
A manager from Holland
An Irish journalist called Fynn
Everybody on the planet
Join in, shout, cheer, stand up
It only happens every four years
It's the one and only . . . World Cup!

Miles Cain

Shoot-out

I'd so like to boot out
The penalty shoot-out
Let the game run on instead
Till someone scores or drops down dead

Colin West

Half-time Pie

What else you gonna do
With that leftover stew
And those cuts of meat you can't identify?
Ingredients of this sort
Just taste better under short – crust
You'll always get a guy with a half-time pie

John Cooper Clarke

The Name of the Game

My first is in ref and twice in offside.
My second's in throw-in and twice in boot.
My third is in scored, but not in saved
My fourth is in penalty and in shoot.
My fifth's twice in dribble, but not in kick.
My sixth is in transfer, but not in fee.
My seventh is in World, but not in Cup.
My eighth is in goal – to play you need me!

John Foster

Give in?

Answer: football

Another One of Those Classic Brazilian Commentary Moments!

GOOOOOOO
OOOOOOOOO
OOOOOOOOOO
OOOOOOOOOOO
OOOOOOOOOOOOO
OOOOOOOOOOOOOO
OOOOOOOOOOOOOOO
OOOOOOOOOOOOOOOO
OOOOOOOOOOOOOOOOO
OOOOOOOOOOOOOOOOOO
OOOOOOOOOOOOOOOOOOO
OOOOOOOOOOOOOOOOOOOO
OOOOOOOOOOOOOOOOOOOOO
OOOOOOOOOOOOOOOOOOOOOO
OOOOOOOOOOOOOOOOOOOOOOO
OOOOOOOOOOOOOOOOOOOOOOOO
OOOOOOOOOOOOOOOOOOOOOOOOO
OOOOOOOOOOOOOOOOOOOOOOOOOOAL!

Graham Denton

JUBilation

The shot's curled in,
The shirt's gone up,
The hands outstretched,
The kneeling slide,
The winning goal,
Yeah, victory glide!

Phil Burrell

Frightening But True

It's embarrassing, ridiculous
It's frightening, it's sad!
But my mum's a better footballer
Than my brother, me
And Dad!

Ian Bland

I'm for . . .

I'm for the team that's fast and clean
not dirty or mean. I'm for the team
that doesn't stop running
whose passes are stunning
and the ball seems to know
just where it should go
to fall smooth and neat
at the next twitching feet

as they sweep down the pitch
switching wings as they race
to make space or run rings
round an outpaced defence. I'm for
the team whose strength is skill,
that will twist and swerve
with control and nerve
as they dribble through the middle
but don't fiddle, fight or quibble
with the ref
wasting time and breath. I'm
for the team who play so well
that my mind and heart
are lost in their art
so I don't scream or yell
but gasp in delight and grin.
(I don't care if they win.)

Dave Calder

Best of All

I'm Rooney. I'm Neville.
I'm Beckham. I'm James.
I'm Ferdinand, Lampard,
on top of their games.

Some days I am Robinson,
Gerrard or Terry.
I tower like Crouch
and I dribble like Barry.

I'm Owen – unstoppable –
France '98.
No matter the time
or the team, I am great.

I play with my dad
and we fly back in time.
He's Banks and I'm Hurst
at the peak of our prime.

We dazzle the crowds
with our skills and our grins.
And, best of all, England
unfailingly wins.

Ted Scheu

Today We Beat Brazil

Today we beat Brazil ten nil
Ten nil
Ten nil
Today we beat Brazil ten nil
And our striker is a dog

The game with Poland was called off
And we were winning
Seven three
The game with Poland was called off
Cos our striker burst the ball

Tomorrow we play Italy
Italy
Italy
Tomorrow we play Italy
If we can find a ball

We're going to win the World Cup
World Cup
World Cup
We're going to win the World Cup
All we need's a ball

(And a new striker who is not a Border Collie
    dog.)

Roger Stevens

Then the Brazilians Turned Up

(with their bicycle kicks, dummies, curlers,
nutmegs, back-heels, feints, shimmies,
swerves . . .)

Football used to be a game
played with the feet and the head.

Then the Brazilians turned up
and left everyone for dead.

They dribbled like the wind.
They played with the hips and the heart.

Football used to be a game.
The Brazilians turned it into an art.

Sean Taylor

Goalkeeper

I patrol my goal from side to side
Like some demented spider
I leap to keep my net secure
But the goal keeps growing wider

John Kitching

Winning the Cup

There's going to be peace on Earth
That's no word of a lie
England will win the World Cup
And rhinoceroses will fly

Roger Stevens

World Cup Fever

My mind keeps wandering, I can't sit still.
Arms waving in the air. I think I'm ill.
My pulse is racing, I feel unwell.
I've been struck down by a football spell.
But I'm not really sure if it is that either,
Perhaps it's a dose of World Cup Fever.

My throat is dry, my voice is hoarse,
My temperature's rising as the game runs its
    course.
I feel like the crossbar has landed on my head.
What diagnosis would explain this instead?
I'm gnawing the goalposts like a hungry
    beaver,
It looks like a case of World Cup Fever.

My face is coloured like the national flag,
My energy levels have begun to sag.
I see facts and figures before my eyes.
'It's a case of match statistics,' the doctor cries,
'And you're singing your heart out like a disco
    diva.
It's a terrible case of World Cup Fever!'

Chris Ogden

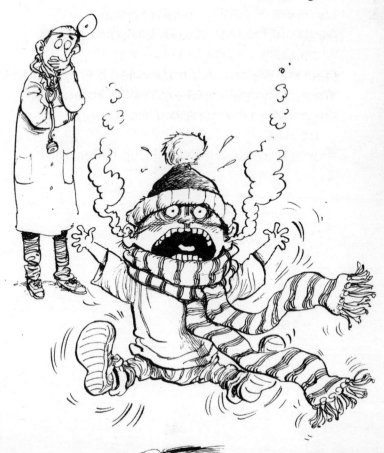

In Praise of Pickles

Scotland Yard baffled, the government too
Who had an answer, who had a clue?
The World Cup was stolen, lost in thin air
All of the country racked with despair
But one hero found it, as everyone knows
A hero who simply followed his nose
There on the outskirts of Old London Town
Pickles the pooch, a hound of renown
Sniffed out the cup from its hiding place
Wagging his tail and solving the case
England then won it, four–two was the score
And we can thank Pickles for evermore.

David Harmer

The First Friendly
(for Private Edward Salter,* Royal Artillery)

The pitch was all cratered and muddy,
Home-made ball not really round,
Their goalposts were two pairs of rifles
Stuck bayonet end in the ground.

The supporters all mixed in together
And they cheered no matter who scored
And nobody cared who was winning
Because footy's a game not a war.

The final whistle was shellfire
So both sides, scattering, ran
Back to their own line of trenches
Each end of no-man's-land
But they never forgot that first friendly
Where the World Cup really began . . .

Kevin McCann

*Who was wounded and honourably discharged
in 1917 and went on to become my grandad.

Cinquain Of Pain

Losing
Bitter defeat
A bad taste in my mouth
A lump in my tired, hoarse throat,
Swallow

Coral Rumble

England's Rock

Bobby Moore was fabulous
Bobby Moore was swell
Bobby Moore was poetry
He read the game so well.

Bobby Moore was magical
Bobby Moore was proud
Bobby Moore had everything
The darling of the crowd.

Bobby Moore was
   masterly
Bobby Moore was
   keen
Bobby Moore was
   captain
Of our World Cup
   winning team.

Richard Caley

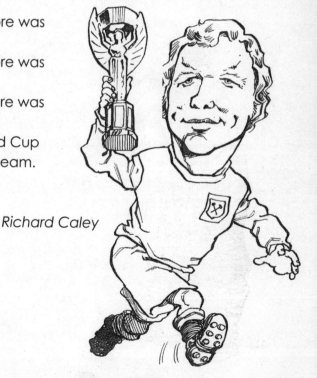

The Dream Team

We are the Dream Team –
We're all football stars

Peter is Pelé
With knees full of scars

Kate's Maradona
(Her fingers are long)

Mark's Bobby Charlton
(He's wiry and strong)

Josie's the tallest
So she's Peter Crouch

Josh is George Best
(Though he walks with a slouch)

Robbie is Beckham
Our best shot by miles

But I have the happiest
Gappiest smiles

And two front teeth missing –
So I'm NOBBY STILES

Clare Bevan

45

FANS: United We Stand

We are the fans who congregate
Behind the goal to celebrate.

We are the fans who will en masse
Cheer every shot, clap every pass.

We are the fans both young and old
Who come each week and brave the cold.

We are the fans who fill the ground
With thunderous noise, oh what a sound.

We are the fans, some black, some white
Who support their teams both day and night.

We are the fans from East and West
Who always think their club the best.

We are the fans who live football
United we stand and united we fall.

We're football crazy
We're football mad
We are the fans who follow our teams
Through good times and through bad.

Richard Caley

Riddle

Many men had hoped to mould me
Many men desire to hold me
No one man can ever win me
There's a streak of gypsy in me
I will go where fortune calls me
Careless of what fate befalls me
Carrying the earth above me
If you love gold, you will love me.

What am I ?

Sue Cowling

Answer: The FIFA World Cup

Penalty

The crowd was still.
The day was hot.
I placed the ball
On the penalty spot.

I licked my lips
My throat was dry.

I booted the ball
Nine miles too high!

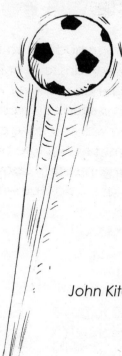

John Kitching

Here We Go

Got to win
Can't lose
Great team
Great news
Put the ball
In the net
Beat the world?
You bet.
Eng-er-land
Slick and fast
World Cup
At last
Waited years
For this to be
No dream
Victory
Eng-er-land
Got to win
Here we go
Let's begin
Eng-er-land
Are the best
Better
Than the rest
World Cup
Here we go

Win it? YES!
Or is that . . . ?

David Harmer

The World's Best

My dad's the world's best,
He's a football referee.
He referees World Cup matches
From a seat on our settee.

An hour before the kick-off
He gets changed into his kit.
He then inspects the room
And tells us where to sit.

As we watch the pre-match build-up
He waits beside the door
Until the teams come out,
Then he strides across the floor.

He stands to attention
While the national anthems play,
Then takes his seat on the settee
As the game gets under way.

His eagle eyes spot every foul
The opposition makes.
He's very quick to point out
The real ref's mistakes.

He won't stand for any nonsense.
On dissent he's very hard.
If we challenge his decisions
He shows us a red card.

But sometimes he forgets
His self-appointed role
By letting out a mighty roar
When England scores a goal.

John Foster

Penalty Thoughts
(choose your own ending)

This is it then –
It's down to me:
The game hangs on
This penalty.

Score and we lift
The World Cup;
Miss and we're only
Runners-up.

Keeper looks huge –
Had a brilliant game.
Only wish I
Could say the same.

He's confident . . .
Jigging about,
Doing his best
To freak me out.

Go for the corner . . .
Which one though?
Strike it sweetly,
Keep it low.

Left corner? No . . .
Which side? Which side?
Last one I took
Went miles wide.

Just remember:
Keep it low.
Clean off the studs.
Here we go . . .

End of a dream . . .
The save was good.   **OR**   Blazed it high:
There'll be sympathy.   It's a no-win . . .
My name is mud.   Scraped the bar –
                                And went in!

Eric Finney

Twenty Words About Brazil

Samba dancing
Midriffs flashing
Dream smashing
Goalies crashing
Shirt swinging
Free kicks zinging
World Cup winning
Carnival kings
From Brazil

Andy Tooze

A Sporting Supporter

'I don't mind wearing the stripy socks,
The red, the white and the blue.

'I don't mind wearing the waxy paints,
Although they stick like glue.

'I don't mind wearing the slinky scarf,
Although it twists and tangles.

'I don't mind wearing the floppy shorts,
Although the drawstring dangles.

'I don't mind wearing the baggy shirt,
Although it's miles too big,

'But NOBODY,' grumbles our Grandma,
'Can make me wear that WIG.'

Clare Bevan

The Win Within

Sweden
Canada
Poland
Italy
Argentina
The Bahamas
Netherlands

Our victory lands within the defeat of other
    nations

Lisa Watkinson

A Bit Soon?

I want to be a World Cup star
I want to be the best
I want to score a million goals
With England on my chest

I want to hear the cheering crowds
But p'raps I'll have to wait
I might be rushing things a bit
After all, I'm only eight . . .

Clive Webster

Same Again As Sixty-Six

With GERRARD on her shoulders
Gran sits in her England shirt
Cracking her rattle on her husband's head
'What time's kick-off, Bert?'

Howard Peach

The Art of World Cup Football

Brazil and Paraguay drew,
England and Germany coloured in

Tim Hopkins

Football in the Living Room

Bounce! Bump! Spin! Crash!
Vase wobble! Fall! Smash!
Shoot! Score! Blast! Boom!

FOOTBALL IN THE LIVING ROOM!

Dive! Stretch! Tip! Jerk!
TV dented! Will not work!
Throw! Kick! Swerve! Zoom!

FOOTBALL IN THE LIVING ROOM!

Trap! Drive! Goal! YES!
Deep trouble! House mess!
Parent trouble! Double gloom!

KICKED OUT OF THE LIVING ROOM!

Ian Bland

The First Torres

19th July 1966, Goodison Park, Everton

Portugal 3 Brazil 1 (Group 3 Qualifying Round)

Over 60,000 people and I was one of them.
Scouse - the minority language that night as
both sets of supporters
roared their sides on in Portuguese.

World Champions Brazil,
their shirts the colour of last night's brilliant
    custard.
Portugal's glowed like the glazed cherries we
    had at Christmas.

Brazil had Pelé – Portugal had Eusébio
as well as the tallest player
I'd ever seen, José Augusto Torres,
2.04 metres high – that's over 6 feet 6 inches
if you're reading this to your grandad.

Torres was part tower block and part giraffe,
everything in the air was his.

A pigeon flew over the Gwladys Street end
    Torres headed it on to Eusébio;

it was that kind of night
when football waved its wand over us,
and a 'good giant' leaped
like a swan on a trampoline,
and every ball in the sky was his personal
    spinning planet . . .

. . . as the World Champions became small in
the long shadow of the First Torres.

Stewart Henderson

Nineteen Sixty-six

July 30th, Wembley Stadium
Proud in red and white
Alf Ramsey's wingless wonders
Courageous in the fight
Hurst the hat-trick hero
Banks between the sticks
The glory of the story
Nineteen sixty-six

Cohen, strong, unbeatable
Wilson, sharp and in control
Big Jack towers at the back
Moore, the faultless Captain's
    role
The English Pelé – Charlton
The magic match and mix
The grinning of the winning
Nineteen sixty-six

Peters, quiet, studious
Ball runs miles and
    miles
Hunt the perfect
    predator
Nobby's toothless
    smiles

All for one and one for all
Everything just clicks
Forty years of cheers
Nineteen sixty-six

Losing, winning, drawing
A game of highs and lows
The theatre of extra time
The goals, the ebbs and flows
They think that it's all over
Some fans are on the pitch
Glorious, victorious
Nineteen sixty-six

It will never be all over
Everything just fits
History we witnessed
The famous crimson kits
4–2 the magic scoreline
Putting on the Ritz
Forever we'll remember
All the twists and kicks
England, champions of the world
Nineteen sixty-six

Paul Cookson

The World in a Cup

The World in a Cup
from which you can sup
hat-tricks and free kicks and dreams
a deliberate trip
a delicate chip
a fellowship of all the best teams.

The World in a Cup
from which you can sup
enjoying the taste and the smell
of an African night
and the joy and delight
of watching your team winning well.

The World in a Cup
from which you can sup
a global fiesta of skill
with the Final desire
of the Three Lions on fire –
England four versus Someone Else – Nil.

Stewart Henderson

The Best Player in the World Was a Goalkeeper

Never mind Pelé or Diego Maradona
Never mind Charlton or Johan Cruyff.

The best player ever was a goalkeeper
With a name Charles Dickens couldn't have
    improved upon.

What else would you call the man who
    specialized in saving?

Banks.

Gary Boswell

ME and the HAND of GOD

Did
I
Ever
Get
Over
Maradona's
Arm
Rising
Aerially,
Duping
Outrageously?
Not
At all . . .

Mark Roberts

How It Goes

England set off
Full of hope
Till we meet
Someone called Hermann
Cos it always
Goes to penalties
And then we
Lose to the Germans.

Andy Seed

The Grace That Launched a Thousand Hips

(For Johan Cruyff)

No man can turn like Johann can
That swivel, twist and back-heel flips
Defenders dazzled by the turn
We tried to emulate and learn
The grace that launched a thousand hips

The skill that gave us all a thrill
That no one can outshine, eclipse
Inspired us to imitate
Your expertise and twist of fate
The grace that launched a thousand hips

The stuff of folklore, legend or
The moment of World Championships
Forever you will always be
Remembered in our history
The grace that launched a thousand hips

Paul Cookson

Tonight I Played Like Beckham, Today He Played Like Me

England 2 – Greece 2

Tonight I played like Beckham
Today he played like me.
True, I haven't got the skill
And I can't bend it like him.
OK, I didn't score the free kick against Greece
That took us to the World Cup –
Mine went over the hedge into next door's
    greenhouse –
But tonight I played like Beckham
And today he played like me.

It wasn't anything to do with ability
But everything to do with attitude.
He was like the kid on the park,
Anoraks for goalposts,
Wanting to kick every single ball,
Be involved in every single move,
Tackle every single tackle.
His position went out of the window,
He was everywhere,

Left, right, centre, attack and defence,
Like a bee around the honeypot.

And it was because of that,
Because he was once again that kid on the
    park
Who'll play till it's dark,
That kid who'll carry on
Because he doesn't want to lose,
That tonight I played a little bit like Beckham
And today he played a little bit like me.

Except he was better.

Paul Cookson

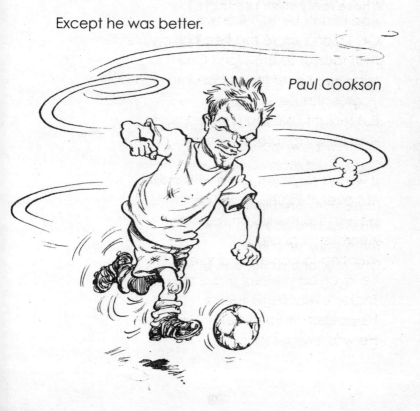

Three Shirts on a Line

It's coming home
It's coming home
It's coming
Football's coming home

Three shirts on a line
Flapping in the breeze
Three shirts on a line
Whose footy shirts are these?

When we were kids we used to play
It seems like yesterday
'E-v-e-r-t-o-n', 'L-i-v-e-r-p-o-o-l'
'Come on T-r-a-n-m-e-r-e'
Hey it was neat, five-a-side in the street
The world it was neat
Cos we remember . . .

Three shirts on a line
Washed and good as new
Three shirts on a line
One red, one white, one blue

Three shirts on a line
Dripping wet and steaming
Three shirts on a line
Reasons to be dreaming

It's coming home
It's coming home
It's coming
Football's coming home.

Roger McGough

Dad - Don't Shout at the Ref!

Always just the same, every single game
I bet that you can hear him in Kiev
Does he have to be so loud? He's louder than
   the crowd
Dad – don't shout at the ref!

His cheeks are burning red, each hair stands off
   his head
Raving without ever taking breath
Yelling and he's screaming and both his ears
   are steaming
Dad – don't shout at the ref!

There's no chance of him stopping, both his
   eyes are popping
Shouting like a bonkers TV chef
Jumping when he rants like there's scorpions
   down his pants
Dad – don't shout at the ref!

Always disagreeing with every thing he's seeing
Every little thing leaves him bereft
Sweating most profusely while his tongue is
   wagging loosely
Dad – don't shout at the ref!

His theory seems to be, it's a conspiracy
Complaining that it might as well be theft
Screaming and he's howling that no one sees
    the fouling
Dad – don't shout at the ref!

Because he's inconsistent, berating the
    assistant
That a fate awaits them both that's worse than
    death
We know his football passion'll make him more
    irrational
Dad – don't shout at the ref!

Mum's partly to blame when she says it's just a
    game
And asks him whether all his sense has left
If he doesn't start to stop it then his heart is
    going to cop it
Dad don't shout – don't let the anger out
It's not what it's about . . .
DAD – DON'T – SHOUT – AT – THE – REF!

Paul Cookson

Fantastic Footy Trivia Quiz

1. How tall is the Jules Rimet trophy?
  a. 20 cm   **b.** 35 cm   **c.** 50 cm

2. Who were the very first winners of the World Cup?
  a. Brazil   **b.** Uruguay   **c.** Italy

3. How many teams qualify for the World Cup Finals?
  a. 32   **b.** 36   **c.** 40

4. The first mascot was used by England in the 1966
World Cup. What was it?
  a. Bulldog   **b.** Lionheart   **c.** World Cup
    Billy   Lenny   Willie

5. Geoff Hurst was the first player to score a hat-trick
in a World Cup Final. He was also the first to do
what in a World Cup Final?
  a. score with a   **b.** receive a   **c.** swap shirts
    header   booking   with opponent

6. In 1994 the World Cup Final was decided by a
penalty shoot-out for the first time. The score was
3–2. Who were the two teams?
  a. Brazil v   **b.** Italy v   **c.** Brazil v
    Uruguay   West Germany   Italy

7. Why was shirt-swapping banned in 1986?
  a. Health and safety
  b. FIFA didn't want the players to 'bare their chests'
  c. FIFA didn't want the players to show off in front
    of the 'ladies'

8. Which is the only team to have appeared in every one of the eighteen Finals tournaments?

a. Brazil **b.** Italy **c.** Uruguay

9. How many goals did Gary Lineker score in the 1986 Finals?

a. 7 **b.** 8 **c.** 6

10. Who was famous for dancing without his teeth in after a World Cup Final win?

a. Pelé **b.** Nobby Stiles **c.** Maradona

11. 1966 England World Cup winners Bobby Moore, Geoff Hurst and Martin Peters played for which team?

a. Tottenham Hotspur **b.** Fulham **c.** West Ham United

12. Which manager took England to the World Cup Semi-final in 1990?

a. Sir Bobby Robson **b.** Terry Venables **c.** Graham Taylor

13. Which player was taken to the 2006 World Cup as a seventeen-year-old?

a. Jermaine Jenas **b.** Theo Walcott **c.** Ashley Young

14. In 2002 David Beckham and Danny Murphy suffered metatarsal injuries. So did a third England player. Who was he?

a. Rio Ferdinand **b.** Gary Neville **c.** Michael Owen

15. Edison Arantes do Nascimento is better known as which player?
a. Maradona   **b.** Ronaldo   **c.** Pelé

16. What is the name of the dog that found the World Cup in 1966?
a. Bobby   **b.** Robbie   **c.** Pickles

17. Who did the 'First Torres' play for?
a. Peru   **b.** Portugal   **c.** Paraguay

18. Which player had a 'turn' named after him?
a. David Beckham   **b.** Pelé   **c.** Johan Cruyff

19. Who was the 'English Pelé'?
a. Bobby Charlton   **b.** Bobby Moore   **c.** Glenn Hoddle

20. Who scored England's first goal against Greece in 2001?
a. David Beckham   **b.** Teddy Sheringham   **c.** Michael Owen

21. Who was famous for celebrating goals with a robotic dance?
a. Jermain Defoe   **b.** Paul Gascoigne   **c.** Peter Crouch

22. The following are anagrams of which England players (past and present)?

- **a.** HARTY BARGER
- **b.** RED VEST RANGER
- **c.** PARK FARM LAND
- **d.** FRIEND IN ROAD
- **e.** I SEEK MY HEEL
- **f.** ROY WON AN EYE
- **g.** DIM BAKED CHAV
- **h.** G! HERO STUFF
- **i.** PRIME NET STAR
- **j.** BEST BOYS NIL
- **k.** ARE GREY LINK
- **l.** A RASH LEANER
- **m.** PURE CROCHET
- **n.** O CASHLY EEL
- **o.** BOMBER BOYO
- **p.** LINES JAMMER
- **q.** HI LOW MENACE
- **r.** SAD NAME DIVA
- **s.** FA COOP – LIABLE

Can you think of any more?

A selected list of titles available from Macmillan Children's Books

The prices shown below are correct at the time of going to press. However, Macmillan Publishers reserves the right to show new retail prices on covers, which may differ from those previously advertised.

Paul Cookson

I'd Rather Be a Footballer	978-0-330-45713-2	£4.99
Give Us a Goal!	978-0-330-43654-0	£3.99
Pants on Fire	978-0-330-41798-3	£4.99
The Truth About Teachers	978-0-330-44723-2	£4.99
The Truth About Parents	978-0-330-47733-8	£5.99
The Works	978-0-330-48104-5	£7.99

All Pan Macmillan titles can be ordered from our website, www.panmacmillan.com, or from your local bookshop and are also available by post from:

Bookpost, PO Box 29, Douglas, Isle of Man IM99 1BQ

Credit cards accepted. For details:
Telephone: 01624 677237
Fax: 01624 670923
Email: bookshop@enterprise.net
www.bookpost.co.uk

Free postage and packing in the United Kingdom